FIRST 50 SONGS
YOU SHOULD PLAY ON THE VIOLIN

ISBN 978-1-5400-0433-8

7777 W. BLUEMOUND RD. P.O. BOX 13819 MILWAUKEE, WI 53213

Visit Hal Leonard Online at
www.halleonard.com

ALL OF ME

VIOLIN

Words and Music by JOHN STEPHENS
and TOBY GAD

ALL YOU NEED IS LOVE

VIOLIN

Words and Music by JOHN LENNON
and PAUL McCARTNEY

AMAZING GRACE

VIOLIN

Traditional American Melody

BASIN STREET BLUES

VIOLIN

Words and Music by
SPENCER WILLIAMS

(small notes optional)

BEST SONG EVER

Violin

Words and Music by EDWARD DREWETT,
WAYNE HECTOR, JULIAN BUNETTA
and JOHN RYAN

CANON IN D

VIOLIN

By JOHANN PACHELBEL

CARNIVAL OF VENICE

VIOLIN

By JULIUS BENEDICT

Moderately, with motion

CIRCLE OF LIFE
from THE LION KING

VIOLIN

Music by ELTON JOHN
Lyrics by TIM RICE

DUST IN THE WIND

VIOLIN

Words and Music by
KERRY LIVGREN

EVERMORE
from BEAUTY AND THE BEAST

VIOLIN

Music by ALAN MENKEN
Lyrics by TIM RICE

ELEANOR RIGBY

VIOLIN

Words and Music by JOHN LENNON
and PAUL McCARTNEY

FIGHT SONG

VIOLIN

Words and Music by RACHEL PLATTEN
and DAVE BASSETT

FLY ME TO THE MOON
(In Other Words)

Violin

Words and Music by
BART HOWARD

THE FOOL ON THE HILL

Words and Music by JOHN LENNON
and PAUL McCARTNEY

VIOLIN

GOD BLESS AMERICA®

VIOLIN

Words and Music by
IRVING BERLIN

THE GODFATHER
(Love Theme)
from the Paramount Picture THE GODFATHER

VIOLIN

By NINO ROTA

Slowly and expressively

HALLELUJAH

VIOLIN

Words and Music by
LEONARD COHEN

HAPPY
from DESPICABLE ME 2

Words and Music by
PHARRELL WILLIAMS

VIOLIN

Moderately fast

HELLO

VIOLIN

Words and Music by
LIONEL RICHIE

HELLO, DOLLY!

from HELLO, DOLLY!

Violin

Music and Lyric by
JERRY HERMAN

HOW DEEP IS YOUR LOVE

from the Motion Picture SATURDAY NIGHT FEVER

VIOLIN

Words and Music by BARRY GIBB,
ROBIN GIBB and MAURICE GIBB

THE HUSTLE

Violin

Words and Music by
VAN McCOY

I WILL ALWAYS LOVE YOU

VIOLIN

Words and Music by
DOLLY PARTON

Moderately slow

JESU, JOY OF MAN'S DESIRING

VIOLIN

English Words by ROBERT BRIDGES
Music by JOHANN SEBASTIAN BACH

THE IRISH WASHERWOMAN

VIOLIN

Irish Folksong

JUST GIVE ME A REASON

Violin

Words and Music by ALECIA MOORE,
JEFF BHASKER and NATE RUESS

JUST THE WAY YOU ARE

VIOLIN

Words and Music by BRUNO MARS,
ARI LEVINE, PHILIP LAWRENCE,
KHARI CAIN and KHALIL WALTON

LET IT GO
from FROZEN

VIOLIN

Music and Lyrics by KRISTEN ANDERSON-LOPEZ
and ROBERT LOPEZ

MAS QUE NADA

VIOLIN

Words and Music by
JORGE BEN

MY HEART WILL GO ON
(Love Theme from 'Titanic')
from the Paramount and Twentieth Century Fox Motion Picture TITANIC

VIOLIN

Music by JAMES HORNER
Lyric by WILL JENNINGS

NIGHT TRAIN

VIOLIN

Words by OSCAR WASHINGTON
and LEWIS C. SIMPKINS
Music by JIMMY FORREST

41

PURE IMAGINATION
from WILLY WONKA AND THE CHOCOLATE FACTORY

VIOLIN

Words and Music by LESLIE BRICUSSE
and ANTHONY NEWLEY

ROAR

VIOLIN

Words and Music by KATY PERRY,
MAX MARTIN, DR. LUKE,
BONNIE McKEE and HENRY WALTER

ROLLING IN THE DEEP

VIOLIN

Words and Music by ADELE ADKINS
and PAUL EPWORTH

SATIN DOLL

VIOLIN

By DUKE ELLINGTON

THEME FROM "SCHINDLER'S LIST"

from the Universal Motion Picture SCHINDLER'S LIST

VIOLIN

Music by JOHN WILLIAMS

SHAKE IT OFF

VIOLIN

Words and Music by TAYLOR SWIFT,
MAX MARTIN and SHELLBACK

SEE YOU AGAIN

from FURIOUS 7

VIOLIN

Words and Music by CAMERON THOMAZ,
CHARLIE PUTH, JUSTIN FRANKS
and ANDREW CEDAR

STAND BY ME

VIOLIN

Words and Music by JERRY LEIBER,
MIKE STOLLER and BEN E. KING

THE STAR-SPANGLED BANNER

Violin

Words by FRANCIS SCOTT KEY
Music by JOHN STAFFORD SMITH

STAY WITH ME

VIOLIN

Words and Music by SAM SMITH,
JAMES NAPIER, WILLIAM EDWARD PHILLIPS,
TOM PETTY and JEFF LYNNE

STOMPIN' AT THE SAVOY

Violin

By BENNY GOODMAN,
EDGAR SAMPSON and CHICK WEBB

Bright Swing

SUMMERTIME

from PORGY AND BESS®

VIOLIN

Music and Lyrics by GEORGE GERSHWIN,
DuBOSE and DOROTHY HEYWARD
and IRA GERSHWIN

A TASTE OF HONEY

VIOLIN

Words by RIC MARLOW
Music by BOBBY SCOTT

TENNESSEE WALTZ

VIOLIN

Words and Music by REDD STEWART
and PEE WEE KING

TURKEY IN THE STRAW

VIOLIN

American Folksong

TEQUILA

VIOLIN

By CHUCK RIO

UPTOWN FUNK

Violin

Words and Music by MARK RONSON,
BRUNO MARS, PHILIP LAWRENCE, JEFF BHASKER, DEVON GALLASPY,
NICHOLAUS WILLIAMS, LONNIE SIMMONS, RONNIE WILSON,
CHARLES WILSON, RUDOLPH TAYLOR and ROBERT WILSON

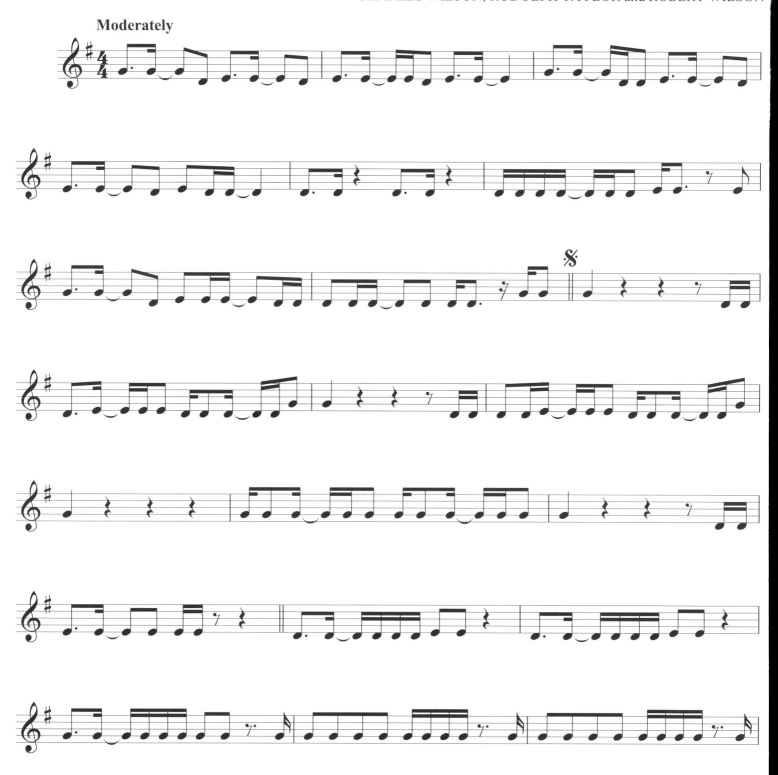

VIVA LA VIDA

Violin

Words and Music by GUY BERRYMAN,
JON BUCKLAND, WILL CHAMPION
and CHRIS MARTIN

YOU RAISE ME UP

VIOLIN

Words and Music by BRENDAN GRAHAM
and ROLF LOVLAND